# I feel Anxious

Written & illustrated by
*Sharon Shannon*

© Copyright 2021

Hi, my name is Ellie.
This book is to help other kids like me.
I find it helps to know we're not alone,
And that others are in the same zone.

Some days I have a funny feeling in my tummy,
I decided to talk about it with Mummy.
She said to describe what way it feels,
I said, 'it sort of feels like butterflies doing cart-wheels'.

Sometimes it feels like a tummy ache,
Other times I feel worried when I wake.
Some days I don't want to go to school or go out.
I don't know what these feelings are all about.

'Talking about your worries is always good', Mum replied.
'We shouldn't keep our feelings all cooped up inside!
You did the right thing talking to me,
I will help you find out what it could be'.

'We'll talk to the Doctor to check everything is Okay,
I'll phone and see if they can see us today'.
Dr Buttercup was lovely and kind,
She asked about what was happening in my mind.

She said I have a thing called ANXIETY,
There is more than one sign, there's a whole variety!
It is natural to feel worried sometimes,
Everyone does and that's just fine!

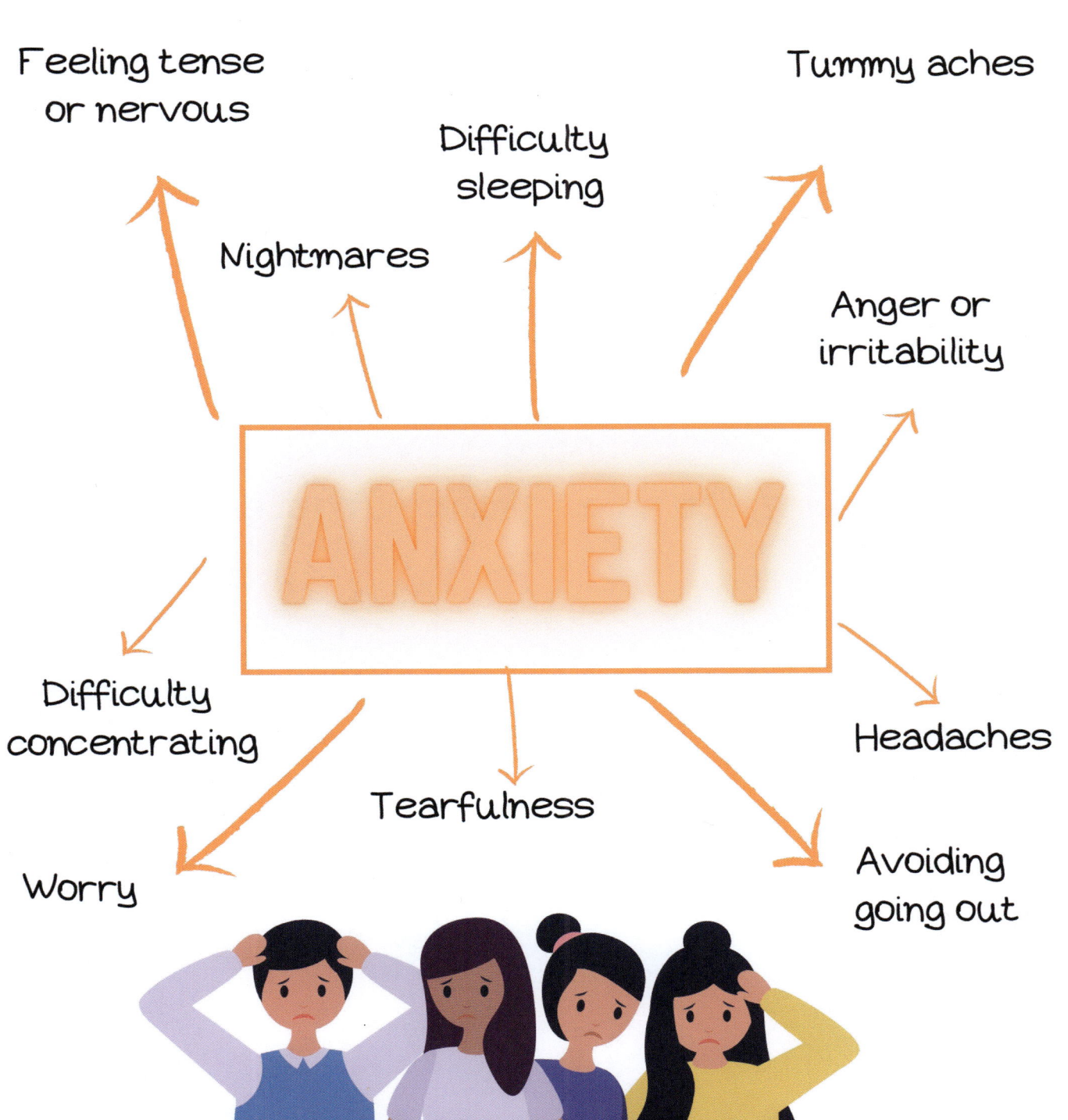

There are things to do and activities to try,
All aimed at helping me to understand why.
Lots of things make me feel worried, some big, others small.
But Mum and the Dr said we can overcome them all

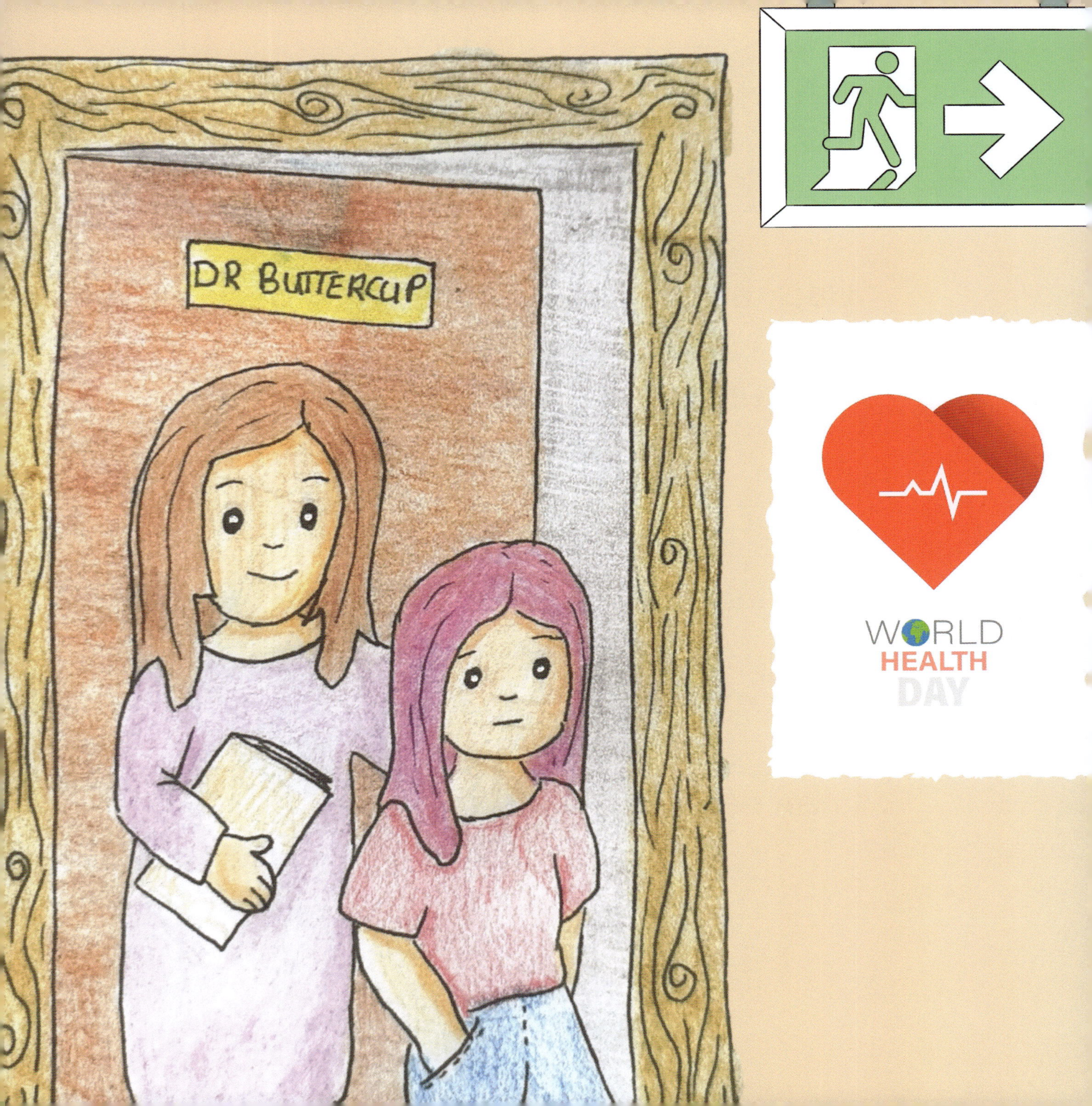
DR BUTTERCUP
WORLD
HEALTH
DAY

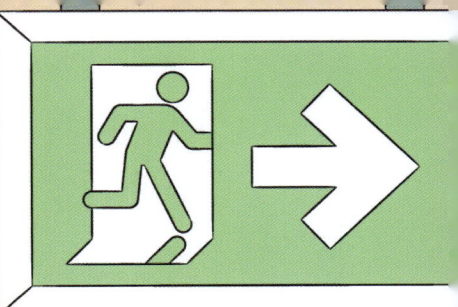

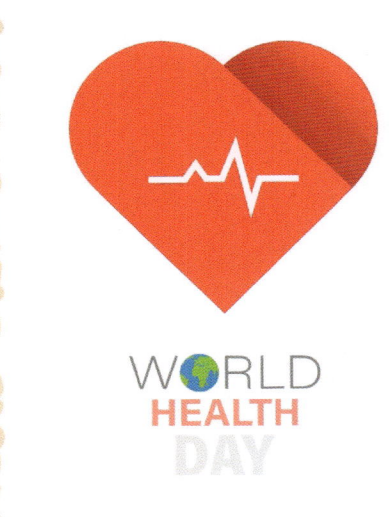

Back at home we set to work trying things the Dr said.
The first one helps to organise the thoughts in my head.
I took a notebook and started to draw and write,
Getting all my worries out helps me feel less uptight.
I'm going to Journal and draw every day,
I can really express myself this way.

Talking with someone you trust was also advised,
It can be a parent, a teacher or any grown up who's wise.
Talking about my worries helps me to see,
That things aren't always as bad as they seem.
A trusted adult can help me find a solution,
And realise that all problems have a resolution.

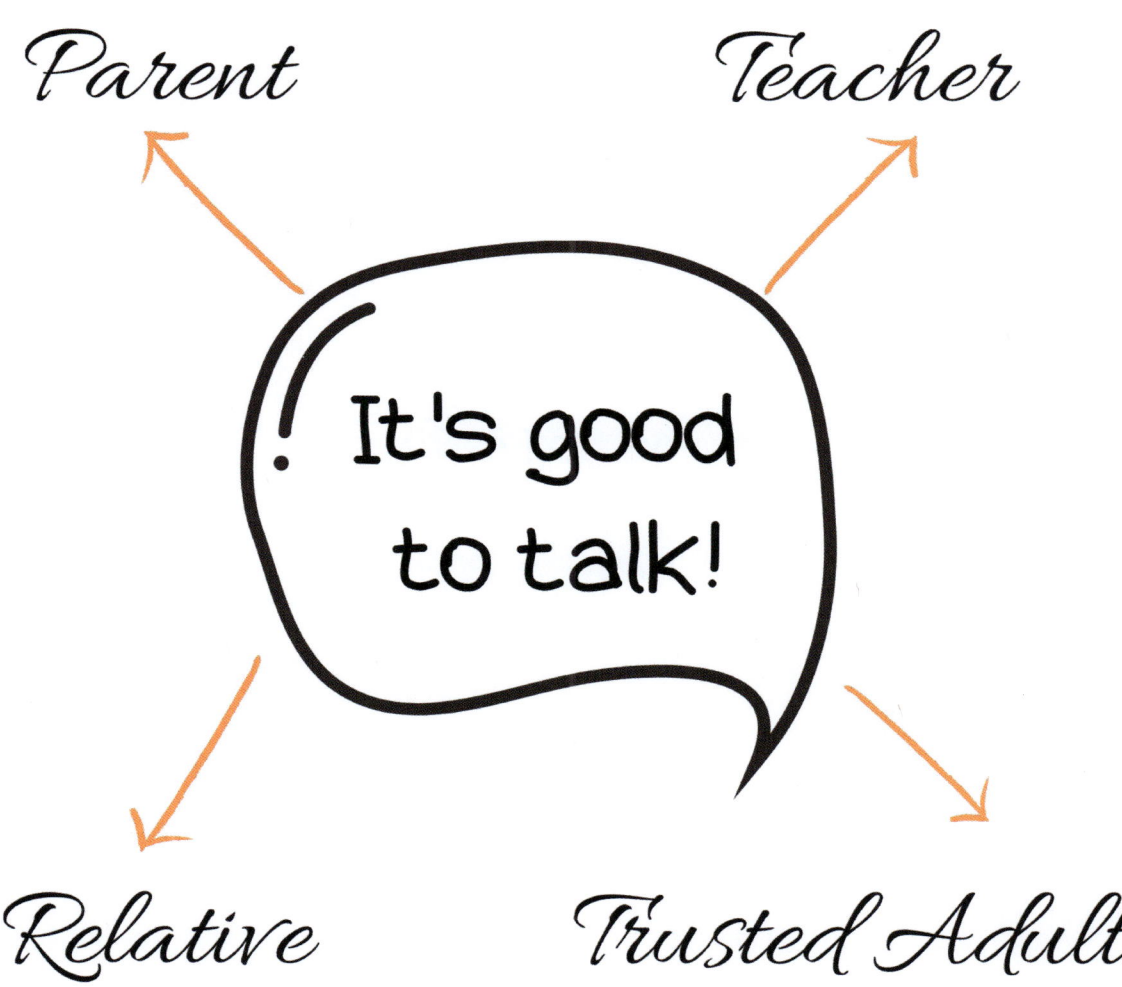

When I share my problems, they seem less of a burden,
And it helps me to feel less stressed and uncertain.
There is an old saying mum told me to remember on life's path.
-A problem shared is a problem halved!

Another trick I am going to try is
breathing deeply in and
out,
10 times in and 10 times out slowly and
calmly is what it's
all about!
This breathing helps relaxation,
It takes a bit of concentration.
You can do it absolutely anywhere,
Whether at home, school or in the open
air.

I spend my spare time playing with my pets,
I have 4 dogs and a grumpy cat I can't forget!
Animals are so relaxing and really help when I feel stressed out,
They really understand me and are loyal friends without a doubt.

I also have a little worry doll who helps me sleep all night,
She listens to my worries so is really quite polite!
I place her under my pillow before I turn out the light,
She takes on my anxiety so I can relax until mornings light.

Take a warm bath or shower

Read a good book

Here are some tips and techniques for you.
To try on the days when you are feeling blue.
Do them all or just a few,
Do whatever is helpful and right for you!

Start a gratitude journal

Develop a self care routine

Make a worry box

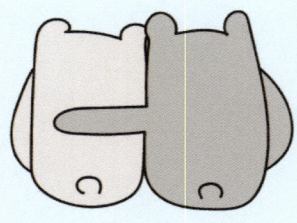
HUG!

Go for a walk

Practice Mindfulness

Guided relaxation audio

Paint or draw

Spend time doing a hobby or start a new one

Do a craft project or make something

Have some alone time in a quiet space

Play with modelling clay or playdough

Practice positive self talk

Use a weighted blanket

Spend time outdoors

Use essential oils to relieve stress

Use a stress ball

Do some Yoga poses

Listen to music

Do a puzzle or play a game

# FUN BREATHING ACTIVITY

Think of your favourite hot food, mine is pizza! In your mind imagine you are holding the food in your hand and smelling it as you breathe in through your nose slowly counting to 5. Then blow on the food to cool it down by breathing out through your mouth again slowly counting to 5. Repeat several times until you feel calm

# VISUALISATION ACTIVITY

Think of what is worrying you. Concentrate on one thing at a time. Visualise it as a setting on a dial, in your mind slowly turn the dial down as you breathe slowly and calmly

# RELAXATION TECHNIQUE

Find a quiet space and get comfortable. Close your eyes and take a few steady breaths.

Imagine yourself in a beautiful place, it could be a beach, or a wood, a mountain or meadow.

Relax your body and feel the warmth from the sun, listen to the gentle breeze in the trees and the cheerful birdsong. Smell the flowers and grass, or listen to the ocean and the sound of each wave. The more senses you can include, the more vivid and real the image will feel. Think about the sights and sounds, feelings and smells for 5 to 10 minutes or until you feel relaxed.

Assure yourself that you can return to this place of serenity anytime you wish to relax.

Open your eyes and re-join the world around you.

Repeat as needed!

Some of our other titles available on Amazon

Find us on
## facebook
Lemur Lane Books

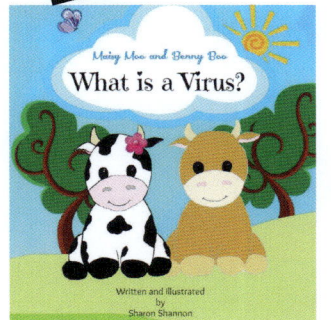

Printed in Great Britain
by Amazon